W9-AEE-051

Hank
AARON

HANK AARON
Groundbreaking Baseball Slugger

by Doug Williams

Published by ABDO Publishing Company, PO Box 398166, Minneapolis, MN 55439. Copyright © 2014 by Abdo Consulting Group, Inc. International copyrights reserved in all countries. No part of this book may be reproduced in any form without written permission from the publisher. SportsZone™ is a trademark and logo of ABDO Publishing Company.

Printed in the United States of America,
North Mankato, Minnesota
102013
012014

Editor: Chrös McDougall
Series Designer: Christa Schneider

Library of Congress Control Number: 2013946583

Cataloging-in-Publication Data

Williams, Doug.
 Hank Aaron: groundbreaking baseball slugger / Doug Williams.
   p. cm. -- (Legendary athletes)
 Includes bibliographical references and index.
 ISBN 978-1-62403-127-4
 1. Aaron, Hank, 1934- --Juvenile literature.   2. Baseball players--United States--Biography--Juvenile literature. 3. African American baseball players--United States--Biography--Juvenile literature. 1. Title.
 796.357/092--dc23
 [B]

                                        2013946583

TABLE OF CONTENTS

Henry Aaron crushes his 715th career home run on April 8, 1974, breaking Babe Ruth's hallowed record.

The New King

As Henry Aaron stepped into the batter's box on the night of April 8, 1974, he felt the weight of the world upon his shoulders. For almost two years, Aaron had been closing in on baseball's record for career home runs. He was exhausted by the chase and tired of answering questions about it. And he was sickened by the hateful letters and death threats he had received because he was an African American trying to break the record of a white superstar.

Yet even while under tremendous pressure, and at the ages of 39 and 40, Aaron continued to be one of the best hitters in baseball. Now, as he stood at the plate wearing his familiar No. 44 for the Atlanta Braves, Aaron was tied with the great Babe Ruth with 714 home runs.

More than 53,000 fans in Atlanta Stadium and a national television audience watched as Aaron focused his gaze on Los Angeles Dodgers pitcher Al Downing. There were no outs with a runner on first base in the bottom of the fourth inning as Aaron methodically took his practice swings.

When the left-handed Downing delivered his first pitch, it was low and in the dirt for ball one. Downing's next pitch was a high fastball, right over the plate. It was the kind of pitch Aaron had been crushing for 20 years in the major leagues. So Aaron swung, whipping his bat through the strike zone with his powerful arms and wrists. In an instant, the ball rocketed on a high arc toward left-center field.

Dodgers left fielder Bill Buckner and center fielder Jimmy Wynn raced back to the outfield fence as they tracked the ball, converging near the 385-foot sign. Buckner climbed the fence in a vain attempt to catch the ball, but it sailed far over his head.

"A Marvelous Moment"

Hall of Fame broadcaster Vin Scully did play-by-play for the Braves-Dodgers game the night of April 8, 1974. His call of Aaron's 715th home run captured not only the excitement of the moment, but its place in history. "There's a high drive into deep left-center field. Buckner goes back to the fence, and it's gone!" said Scully, who waited 26 seconds through the sound of fireworks and cheering before adding: "What a marvelous moment for baseball. What a marvelous moment for Atlanta and the state of Georgia. What a marvelous moment for the country and the world. A black man is getting a standing ovation in the Deep South for breaking a record of an all-time idol. And it is a great moment for all of us, particularly for Henry Aaron."[1]

It was a home run, the 715th of Aaron's career. At precisely 9:07 on a chilly night in Georgia, Henry Aaron was the new home run champion of baseball.

As Aaron went into his home-run trot around the bases, the stadium erupted in cheers. Fireworks exploded in the night sky, and the number 715 appeared on a giant message board beyond the center-field fence. By the time he reached second base, the usually stoic Aaron had a big smile as he was congratulated by Dodgers second baseman Davey Lopes and shortstop Bill Russell.

Two enthusiastic young fans jumped onto the field and ran with Aaron between second and third base, slapping him on the back in jubilation. As Aaron rounded third and headed for home, the entire Braves team was waiting for him.

The game came to a halt as Aaron was first hoisted into the air by his teammates, then congratulated by his wife, Billye, his father, Herbert, his mother, Estella, and the rest of his family. His mother, Aaron said later, gave him the strongest,

A Hitter by Any Name

Aaron preferred to be called Henry rather than Hank, but he was OK with Hank. To the public, he was often known as "Hammerin' Hank" for the way he hammered the baseball. Opposing pitchers sometimes called him "Bad Henry" because they could not get him out. And to all who played with or against him, he was acknowledged as one of the best hitters they'd ever seen. "Henry is a streak hitter," said Dodgers executive and former major league player Fresco Thompson. "He only hits on days ending in *y*."[2]

Aaron holds up the ball that he sent over the wall for his 715th home run as he celebrates with fans at Atlanta Stadium on April 8, 1974.

hardest hug of his life. Then, as Aaron stepped to a microphone to say a few words to the fans, he looked as if the weight he had been carrying for so long had simply evaporated.

"I just thank God it's all over," he said.[3]

Although his home run had been historic, Aaron seemed far more relieved than happy. Baseball's new home run king was eager to step out of the spotlight. For most of his career, he'd been a quiet, splendid player who had been overshadowed by more charismatic stars such as Willie Mays and Mickey Mantle. He looked forward to again just playing baseball without all the attention.

"Right now, it feels like just another home run," he said hours after the Braves had won the game 7–4. "I felt all along if I got a strike I could hit it out. I just wanted to touch all the bases on this one."[4]

Hate Mail and Death Threats

The chase had taken its toll, and Aaron was mentally and spiritually exhausted by the time he hit home run number 715. Though society and baseball had evolved a great deal since Aaron left the Negro Leagues to sign a contract with the Braves organization in 1952, he was subjected to the ugliness of racism as he stalked Ruth's record.

After Aaron hit his 600th home run in 1971, it became apparent to most fans that he would have a shot at the most hallowed record in baseball. Ruth had transformed the game with his power and larger-than-life personality during the 1920s and 1930s. The "Sultan of Swat" had achieved legendary status. Many believed his home run record was unbreakable.

Yet as Aaron passed 600 home runs, he began to get hate mail and death threats from people who did not want Ruth's record to fall to a black man.

"Dear Hank Aaron," read one of the letters. "Retire or die! . . . You'll be in Shea Stadium July 6–8, and in Philly July 9th to 11th. . . . You will die in one of those games. I'll shoot you in one of them."[5]

Read another: "You are [not] going to break this record established by the great Babe Ruth if I can help it. . . . Whites are far more superior than [blacks]. . . . My gun is watching your every black move."[6]

As Aaron continued to play, his life changed. Though thousands of supportive fans filled many stadiums on Braves road trips, countering the nastiness, he had to be cautious. He received a police escort to and from the ballpark and always registered under a false name at hotels. He hired a bodyguard. The Federal Bureau of Investigation (FBI) opened his mail and provided protection for his daughter, who was away at college. In Atlanta, he even stayed in temporary lodging rather than in his home.

Aaron said the stress of the chase and the fear he felt made it the worst part of his long career.

"It should have been the most joyous time of my life," he said years later. "But it was a fishbowl life, hell for two and a half years."[7]

So, as Aaron prepared to play against the Dodgers on April 8 in the Braves' 1974 home opener, he was determined to be patient, get a pitch he could handle, and hit it over the wall.

Four days earlier on April 4, he had tied the record with his 714th home run in the first inning of the season's first game, on the road against the Cincinnati Reds. Now he had a chance to set the record in front of his own fans on a night when the Braves were preparing for something special.

The Home Run Ball

Braves relief pitcher Tom House caught Aaron's 715th home run ball as it sailed into the Atlanta bullpen. "As luck would have it, it came right to me," House said. "I didn't have to move. If I would have stood still, it would have hit me right in the forehead."[8] House ran from the bullpen down to the celebration near home plate and gave the ball to Aaron, who held it aloft for all to see. In thanks for the ball, Aaron later bought House a stereo system.

Al Downing's Place in History

Dodgers pitcher Al Downing was in his twelfth full major league season the night he gave up Aaron's 715th home run. He said before the game it would be no different than any other game he had pitched, but he was wrong. Downing's name is memorable to many fans only because he gave up the home run, yet he won 123 games in his career. Downing always said there was no shame in giving up a home run to Aaron, a hitter he said had no weaknesses.

Aaron's father, Herbert, threw out the ceremonial first pitch. A huge map of the United States in the shape of an American flag was painted on the grass in center field. Famous entertainer Pearl Bailey sang the national anthem. Signs everywhere proclaimed support for Aaron, including one that read, "Move Over Babe."

In his first at-bat of the night in the second inning, Aaron walked. In his next at-bat, he hit the ball 400 feet (122 m) into the baseball record book. His ordeal was over.

Hours later in the clubhouse, after he had received a call of congratulation from President Richard Nixon, Aaron could smile.

"I feel I can relax," he said. "I feel my teammates can relax and I think I can have a great season."[9]

Aaron addresses the media after surpassing Babe Ruth's career home run record during the Braves' 1974 home opener against the Los Angeles Dodgers.

Henry Aaron, shown in 1954, had little money while growing up in Mobile, Alabama.

Humble Beginnings

Henry Louis Aaron was born in Mobile, Alabama, on February 5, 1934. He was the third of Herbert and Estella Aaron's eight children.

When Henry was young, the Aarons lived in a poor section of town called "Down the Bay." Herbert Aaron made approximately $80 a week as a boilermaker's helper for a shipbuilding company. Estella managed their home and the children. Later, the family moved to an area on the outskirts of Mobile called Toulminville. In a time of racial segregation, when blacks were barred from living in certain areas of Mobile, Toulminville was all African American. Young Henry and his brothers and sisters did odd jobs to bring in extra money for the family. Often, Henry picked cotton.

Herbert Aaron loved baseball. He had played the game in his youth against some of the top players in the city and had even started a team called the Whippets. Henry, too, fell in love with the game. He would play every chance he could.

With baseballs hard to come by, he often practiced by using broomsticks to hit bottle caps or balls made from rags.

By the time Henry was a teenager, it was apparent he was a special athlete. He went to Mobile's all-black Central High School and was a fine wide receiver on the football team. He also played shortstop and third base for the baseball team that won the Mobile Negro High School championship his freshman and sophomore seasons. In his junior year he transferred to the Josephine Allen Institute.

Because the school did not have a baseball team, he played for local amateur teams. That meant he was not paid. At the age of 15 he signed to play the infield for a semipro team called the Pritchett Athletics for $3 per game. Later, he played for a better semipro team called the Mobile Black Bears.

It was about this time that Henry decided he wanted to be a big-league ballplayer, in part because of Jackie Robinson of the Brooklyn Dodgers. Robinson had broken baseball's color barrier with the Brooklyn Dodgers in 1947. That meant he became the first black athlete to play in the major leagues in the twentieth century. Later, Robinson occasionally came to Mobile with the Dodgers to play exhibitions against Brooklyn's minor league team, the Bears. The games drew big crowds. In 1950, when Henry was 16, Robinson came to Mobile with several other black stars, including Roy Campanella and Larry Doby, to play the Indianapolis Clowns of the Negro Leagues.

"He was always crazy about playing baseball," Herbert Aaron once said of Henry. "But I'd never thought about him becoming a player until the Brooklyn Dodgers came to Mobile for an exhibition game. I took him out to see the game and he told me that night at the ballpark, 'I'm going to be in the big leagues myself, Daddy, before Jackie Robinson is through playing.'"[1]

The Negro Leagues

Henry's first professional team, the Indianapolis Clowns, was a franchise in the Negro American League. Because major league teams refused to sign black players before 1947, separate teams and leagues specifically for black American and dark-skinned Latin American players were formed in the early twentieth century. Beginning in 1920 with the formation of the eight-team Negro National League, black players began playing for teams such as the Chicago American Giants and Kansas City Monarchs.

Later, other leagues formed. The Negro American League began in 1937. The champions of these leagues would meet in a Negro World Series. The leagues were rich in talented players who eventually would be selected to baseball's Hall of Fame, including Josh Gibson, "Cool Papa" Bell, and Satchel Paige. By the time Aaron signed with the Clowns in 1951, the number of Negro League teams was dwindling. With black players now able to sign with major league teams, there was no longer a need for them.

Off to Professional Baseball

It was while Aaron was playing for the Black Bears that he caught the eye of scout Bunny Downs, who worked for the Indianapolis Clowns of the Negro American League. Downs signed Aaron to a contract for $200 a month on November 20, 1951.

The following spring of 1952, Aaron, 18, was the youngest member of the Clowns. When he joined the team, the right-handed batter hit the way he always had, with an unusual cross-handed grip. His right hand was below his left on the bat. The grip limited Aaron's ability to hit the ball with power. Only Aaron's strong hands and wrists, built up by years of hard work and playing baseball, had allowed him to hit well with the awkward grip. While with the Clowns he learned to hold the bat correctly from owner Syd Pollock.

"The first time I came to bat after that, I held the bat the right way and hit a home run," Aaron said.[2]

By this time, Aaron was a skinny, 6-foot-tall shortstop. He played 26 games for the Clowns in 1952, hitting .366 with five home runs, 33 runs

Marriage

One day in 1953, Aaron was introduced to a young woman named Barbara Lucas who lived near him in Jacksonville, Florida. That night, Lucas decided to attend the Jacksonville Tars' game. She watched Aaron hit a single, a double, and a home run. The two soon began dating, and by October they were married. They would have five children together and be married for 18 years until their divorce in 1971.

batted in (RBIs), and nine stolen bases. Scouts from some major league teams noticed Aaron that summer. On June 14, 1952, the Boston Braves purchased his rights from the Clowns for $10,000. Aaron signed his first contract with a major league organization, for $350 per month.

Soon, Aaron was on his way to the Braves' minor league Class C team in Eau Claire, Wisconsin. The 18-year-old infielder showed he belonged, hitting .336 with nine home runs while being named Northern League Rookie of the Year. It was a year of change for Aaron, who was playing with white players for the first time. But fans in Eau Claire and his teammates were welcoming.

Aaron was then promoted to the Braves' minor league team in Jacksonville, Florida, in the South Atlantic League. Before 1953, the league had been whites-only, but that season Aaron was one of five black players, including two teammates. Despite enduring racial taunts and many times being barred from staying at the same hotel as his white

A Fine Manager

When Aaron joined the Jacksonville Tars in 1953, the Braves knew it would be a difficult year for him. At that time much of the Deep South was segregated. Black players had to use separate facilities from ones used by white teammates. Aaron said manager Ben Geraghty was not only a fine baseball manager that season but he also shielded and protected his players from the worst bigotry. "I guess he was one reason I didn't realize I was crusading, because he crowded out a lot of stuff and never let it get close to me," Aaron said.[3]

teammates, Aaron was again terrific. He also showed the quiet, strong character that would define his career.

"There's only one way to break the color line," he told his teammates. "Play so good they can't remember what color you were before the season started."[4]

Aaron was named the league's Most Valuable Player (MVP) in 1953 after hitting .362 with 125 RBIs, 115 runs scored, and 36 doubles. One writer said that Aaron helped Jacksonville advance toward racial understanding that season.

After the season, Aaron spent the winter playing baseball in Puerto Rico. It was one of the most important learning experiences of his career. While playing for manager Mickey Owen, Aaron learned to play the outfield, where he would play in the major leagues. In addition, Owen took the time to work with Aaron to improve his batting stance and hitting technique. Though Aaron had been a good hitter, he was mostly self-taught. Owen showed him how to be better balanced and get his hands in position to swing. It would help Aaron hit the ball to all fields and achieve success at higher levels.

Aaron finished strong in Puerto Rico as well, hitting .322, third in the league. He was ready for his next step.

Jackie Robinson, shown while with the Negro Leagues' Kansas City Monarchs in 1945, was an inspiration to Aaron.

CHAPTER 3

Henry Aaron made his major league debut in 1954 with the Milwaukee Braves.

Welcome to the Big Leagues

The Braves moved from Boston to Milwaukee in 1953. They went 92–62 in their first season and attracted 1.8 million fans, a National League (NL) record at the time. In hopes of being even better in 1954, the team traded for New York Giants outfielder Bobby Thomson, who had hit 26 home runs the previous season. The plan was for Thomson to be Milwaukee's left fielder.

But on March 13, Thomson broke his ankle sliding into second base during a spring training game. Suddenly, the Braves needed a left fielder.

Having just learned to play the outfield during winter ball in Puerto Rico, the 20-year-old Aaron was put into the lineup the next day in an exhibition game against the Boston Red Sox. In that game at the Braves' spring training home field in Bradenton, Florida, Aaron hit a long home run.

"I cracked one over a row of trailers that bordered the outfield fence," Aaron said. "Hit it so hard that [Red Sox star] Ted Williams came

A Fastball Hitter

Even when Aaron broke into the majors as a 20-year-old, he was a great fastball hitter. Teammates marveled at his ability to hit even the fastest pitches. Said longtime NL pitcher Curt Simmons: "Trying to sneak a fastball past Henry Aaron is like trying to sneak the sunrise past a rooster."[3]

running out from the clubhouse wanting to know who it was that could make a bat sound that way when it struck a baseball."[1]

For the rest of spring training, Braves manager Charlie Grimm kept putting Aaron in left field. When the team finally left Florida, Grimm announced Aaron had won the job. The team signed him to his first major league contract.

On their way north toward the season opener, the Braves played a series of exhibition games against the Brooklyn Dodgers in the South and Midwest. At one stop, in Aaron's hometown of Mobile, Alabama, he had a chance to play on the same field with Jackie Robinson in front of his friends and family. Aaron hit a single and double.

"I hoped my father remembered what I told him when I was 14, that I would be in the big leagues while Jackie was still there," Aaron said.[2]

On April 13, 1954, Aaron went hitless in five at-bats in his first official major league game, a 9–8 loss to the Reds in Cincinnati. Two days later in the Braves' home opener against the St. Louis Cardinals, Aaron got his first major league hit, a double, against pitcher Vic

Raschi. On April 23, Aaron hit his first major league home run, in St. Louis, also against Raschi.

Even at such a young age, Aaron showed he was a major league talent in every way. His first season in the big leagues came to an early end when he broke his ankle on September 5 while sliding into third base on a triple. But before that he batted .280, hit 13 home runs, drove in 69 runs, and played fine defense. He finished fourth in voting for the NL Rookie of the Year Award.

Eclipsed by Moon

Aaron finished fourth in voting for the NL's Rookie of the Year in 1954, getting just one first-place vote. St. Louis Cardinals outfielder Wally Moon, who hit .304, was first, followed by Cubs shortstop Ernie Banks, Braves pitcher Gene Conley, and Aaron, whose season was cut short by injury. Aaron far surpassed Moon over his career but said Moon deserved the award.

Becoming a Star

The next year, the Braves moved Aaron to right field, and he had a great spring. As the Braves broke camp for Milwaukee, the Associated Press reported that Aaron looked so good, he might "burn up the league with his hitting."[4]

Aaron did, indeed. In 1955 he played in 153 of 154 games, hit .314 with 27 home runs, scored 105 runs, and drove in 106. He also was selected to play in the All-Star Game for the first time. It would be the first

Aaron and his wife, Barbara, pose with one-day-old sons Lary, *left*, and Gary at the hospital in 1957.

of what would be a record 25 All-Star Games (there were two All-Star Games each year from 1959 to 1962). In that 1955 game, played at Milwaukee's County Stadium, Aaron came into the game as a pinch runner in the fifth inning, then went 2-for-2 and drove in a run and scored a run in the NL's 6–5 victory. At the end of the season, Milwaukee's fans voted him "Brave of the Year."

The next season would prove to be a breakout season for Aaron, who was just 22 years old in 1956.

Aaron hit .328 to win the NL batting championship. He also led the league in hits (200) and doubles (34). Plus he hit 26 home runs. Aaron finished third in the league's voting for MVP, but he was named *The Sporting News* NL Player of the Year.

More importantly, Aaron had become one of the stars of a great Braves lineup of sluggers that also included future Hall of Fame third baseman Eddie Mathews, left fielder Thomson, and first baseman Joe Adcock. The Braves could pitch, too, with future Hall of Famer Warren Spahn the ace and Lew Burdette right behind him in the starting rotation. That season, the Braves almost won an NL championship for their exuberant fans. For the third straight season, Milwaukee drew more than 2 million in attendance.

The Braves went 92–62 to finish just one game behind the Dodgers in the race for the NL pennant. They went into the final three-game series of the season at St. Louis with a chance to tie or overtake the

Becoming a Dad

Henry and Barbara Aaron became parents in Henry's rookie season of 1954 with Milwaukee when their daughter, Gaile, was born. Henry Jr., their first son, was born in early 1957, followed by twins Gary and Lary (Gary would die as an infant). Another daughter, Dorinda, was born in 1962. Aaron would adopt another daughter, Ceci, when he married his second wife. As a college student when Aaron was chasing Babe Ruth's record, Gaile described her dad not as a "home run machine," but as a "mild-tempered, concerned person with human interests, feeling great concern" for his children.[5]

Dodgers, but lost two close games, one in extra innings. There were no divisions at the time, so the best team in each league's regular season claimed the pennant and went to the World Series.

Though the Braves had come up short, the stage was set for future success. This was a team built to win, and Aaron was ready to help carry his team. After just three years in the big leagues, he was an All-Star and happy to be playing in Milwaukee, where the fans were overjoyed to have baseball.

"Milwaukee was perfect for me," he said. "Any player would have been fortunate to play in front of those fans. Baseball has never seen fans like Milwaukee's in the 1950s and never will again."[6]

Dynamic Duo

When Aaron joined the Milwaukee Braves in 1954, the team already had an established young hitting star in third baseman Eddie Mathews. The year before, Mathews led the NL with 47 home runs. In 1954 and 1955 he hit 40 and 41 home runs, respectively. Mathews and Aaron would play together for 13 seasons and form the best home-run duo in baseball history.

In 1965, their final season together in Milwaukee, Mathews' twenty-eighth home run of the year was the 773rd the two had hit as teammates, surpassing the 772 hit by Babe Ruth and Lou Gehrig with the New York Yankees in the 1920s and 1930s. Eventually, Aaron and Mathews hit 863 home runs together. "We weren't jealous of each other at all," Aaron said of Mathews. "That's one reason we were so successful."[7]

NL president Warren Giles presents Aaron with a silver bat on May 19, 1957. The bat was to honor Aaron as the 1956 batting champion.

Henry Aaron and the Milwaukee Braves came into the 1957 season with expectations of winning a pennant.

Champions

The Braves entered 1957 with high expectations. They immediately got off to a running start. Milwaukee won its first five games. Aaron hit .350 over that span with two home runs.

Aaron started the season hitting second in the batting order in front of Eddie Mathews. But as the season progressed, Braves manager Fred Haney moved Aaron into the fourth spot as the cleanup hitter.

The 1957 Braves were a great team, flirting with first place in the NL early and taking first for good on August 6. They clinched the league championship on September 23. And it was Aaron, 23, who led them as he made the leap to become one of the game's biggest stars.

Aaron in 1957 switched to a lighter bat to increase his bat speed, and the change paid big dividends. He hit a league-leading 44 home runs and also led in RBIs with 132 and runs scored with 118. He hit .322 to finish fourth in the batting race behind St. Louis Cardinals outfielder Stan Musial's .351 average. Had Aaron won the batting title, he would have become the first NL player since 1937 to win the Triple Crown by leading his league in home runs, RBIs, and batting average. As it was, Aaron was voted the NL MVP.

By 1957, Aaron's body had matured and filled out. Though he hardly looked imposing in the batter's box at just under 6 feet tall and 178 pounds, he had big shoulders and was strong across the chest, with a slim, 31-inch (79 cm) waist. That year, Braves trainer Doc Feron said Aaron was built "like a rock."[1]

It was his strong wrists and forearms that drew the attention of those in baseball, however. Aaron was so strong with his hands and wrists he could wait on a pitch longer than most batters, then whip his bat through the strike zone to drive the ball to all fields. Cincinnati manager Birdie Tebbetts said Aaron had the "best wrists in baseball."[2]

Changing Bats

Before 1957, Aaron had used a variety of bats. Often, he didn't even use his own, but borrowed those of his teammates that felt right. The bats he had favored most from the Hillerich & Bradsby Louisville Slugger line in 1955 and 1956 were 35 and 36 inches long (89 and 91.4 cm) and weighed from 33 to 36 ounces (936 to 992 g). In 1957, he began using a 36-inch (91 cm) model that weighed only 32 ounces (907 g). The lighter bat allowed Aaron to generate greater bat speed, which resulted in more home runs. After hitting 27 home runs in 1955 and 26 in 1956, Aaron hit 44 in 1957.

A Smart Hitter

In addition, Aaron in just his fourth big-league season had learned a lot about hitting and the pitchers in his league.

"When he first came up, the pitchers used to fool him once in a while," Braves catcher Del Crandall said. "Now he knows them. He has a tremendous faculty for remembering the pitch that got him out the last time. The next time the same pitcher tries it, Henry's liable to hit it out of the park."[3]

Home Run No. 100

On August 15, 1957, Aaron came to bat in the seventh inning of a game against the Reds at Cincinnati's Crosley Field. He'd already hit the ninety-ninth home run of his career in the first inning, and he now faced left-handed relief pitcher Don Gross. Aaron hit the ball deep over the left-field fence for his 100th career homer. He was only 23. Babe Ruth had been 25 when he hit his 100th home run in 1920.

As the 1957 season played out, Aaron was locked in. In May against the Pittsburgh Pirates he had five hits in one game. The next day he had a double, a triple, and a home run with four RBIs. From June 29 to July 5 he hit seven home runs in eight games. He didn't have the speed and flair of Willie Mays or the charisma of Mickey Mantle, but Aaron was thought by many in baseball to be the game's best hitter. As Reds manager Tebbetts said, "Aaron murders everybody."[4]

On September 23, the Braves needed just one win to clinch the NL pennant and were playing the St. Louis Cardinals in Milwaukee. The game was tied 2–2 in

Gold Glove Outfielder

Though Aaron will always be known for his hitting, he was an excellent fielder. He had good speed and covered the outfield with long, graceful strides. In 1958, he won the first of three consecutive Gold Gloves, which are awarded by Rawlings annually to the best fielders at each position in the NL and AL. In 1958, playing mostly right field but also a few games in center, Aaron made just five errors in 153 games and threw out 12 base runners.

the bottom of the 11th inning when Aaron came to bat with two outs and a runner on. He drilled his forty-third home run of the season over the center-field fence for a 4–2 win. The Braves were NL champions. Aaron's teammates carried him off the field that night. Years later, Aaron said it was the best moment of his career.

Future baseball commissioner Bud Selig, then just a Braves fan, was sitting in the stands that night and said the moment was magical.

"People were crying," Selig recalled. "Nobody wanted to leave the park. It was a scene that to this day, 55 years later, is still so etched in my mind."[5]

The Braves played the New York Yankees, the American League (AL) champion, in the World Series. Though Milwaukee had been called "Bushville" by some in the East because it was a Midwest city with a new team, that team beat the mighty Yankees in seven games. Braves pitcher Lew Burdette was the World Series MVP, beating the Yankees three times, including the final game 5–0 in Yankee Stadium in New York.

Milwaukee Braves players carry Aaron off the field after Aaron's walk-off home run against the St. Louis Cardinals clinched the 1957 NL pennant.

Aaron, though, was the top hitter in the series, getting 11 hits in 28 at-bats for a .393 average with three home runs and seven RBIs.

"Happy days had arrived," Aaron said. "During the celebration downtown [in Milwaukee], fans carried around a huge banner that said: 'Bushville Wins!' The Milwaukee Braves were world champions."[6]

The Braves came right back in 1958 to win another NL pennant, and Aaron played a big role again. He hit .326 with 30 home runs, 109 runs scored, and 95 RBIs. He finished third in the voting for the league's MVP.

The Braves finished eight games ahead of the second-place Pirates. They earned a rematch with the Yankees in the World Series.

This time, however, it was the Yankees that won in seven games. Milwaukee won the first two and led 3–1 after four games, but the Yankees rallied to win three straight, including a 6–2 victory in Milwaukee in Game 7. Aaron batted .333 with four RBIs in the World Series.

"I had nine hits in the Series, and after getting 11 the year before, it made me think about putting together a long history of hitting in the World Series," Aaron said years later. "Little did I know that I would never be in one again."[7] He would play 18 more seasons.

Honored in Mobile

After Aaron helped the Braves win the 1957 World Series, officials in his hometown of Mobile, Alabama, announced it would hold a "Hank Aaron Day" to honor him. Aaron and his wife, Barbara, arrived in town via the train and a band played "Take Me Out to the Ball Game" as they stepped off to a cheering crowd. A limousine took the Aarons to the city's Colored Elks Club, where Mobile's mayor gave Aaron a key to the city.

"I don't know it for a fact, but I expect that I was the first black person to get a key to Mobile," Aaron said later. "It might seem like nothing more than a token, but believe me that was a proud day for all the black people of Mobile—a kid from Toulminville being honored by the mayor himself."[8]

Aaron hits a three-run home run against the New York Yankees in Game 4 of the 1957 World Series.

Henry Aaron hits his twelfth home run of the 1959 season during a May 20 game against the San Francisco Giants.

Taking His Place

Though the Braves had fallen short of a World Series championship the previous season, Aaron began 1959 as if he were going to carry Milwaukee to a championship all by himself.

In the first game of the season, he banged out three hits. The next day, he had two. In game number three he had three more. All through April, Aaron was as hot as an August afternoon. In 14 games he was held hitless just once, and he had 31 hits in 61 at-bats for a .508 batting average. Six of those hits were home runs.

He stayed just as hot into May, putting together a 22-game hitting streak. After going 4-for-5 with a home run against the Philadelphia Phillies on May 22, Aaron was batting .468 with 13 home runs. Now in his sixth season and only 25 years old, Aaron was putting up numbers that had people wondering if he might be able to become the first player to hit .400 for a season since Ted Williams in 1941. Some suggested Aaron might

Aaron vs. Drysdale

During the 1959 season, Aaron hit four home runs off Los Angeles Dodgers pitcher Don Drysdale. It was a trend that would continue throughout their careers. Though Drysdale was one of the best pitchers of his era and would be elected to the Hall of Fame, Aaron hit 17 home runs off him, the most he hit off any pitcher. Early in their careers a feud blossomed between them when Drysdale threw inside on two consecutive pitches, backing Aaron off the plate.

challenge the NL record of 254 hits in a season.

"I've never been in a groove quite like I was at the beginning of 1959," Aaron said.[1]

In June against the Giants in San Francisco, Aaron also did something he'd never done before, hitting three home runs in one game.

Though Aaron didn't hit .400 or break the hits record, 1959 was one of his best seasons. He had 223 hits and won his second batting championship with a .355 average. He also hit 39 home runs.

The Braves, meanwhile, finished the season tied for first with the Los Angeles Dodgers. The Dodgers won the first two games of a best-of-three series, however, to deny Milwaukee its third straight World Series appearance.

Five days after the season, Braves manager Fred Haney resigned. In the previous four seasons under Haney, Milwaukee had finished a very close second twice and won two NL championships and one World

Series. Though it was a great run, many in Milwaukee were disappointed the Braves didn't win more championships, including Aaron.

"Every team has ifs and buts, but that doesn't make it any easier," Aaron said. "It still bothers me that we were able to win two pennants and one World Series with the team we had. We should have won at least four pennants in a row."[2]

"Simply the Best Hitter"

Charlie Dressen was hired as Braves manager for the 1960 season, and Milwaukee again finished in second place, seven games behind the Pittsburgh Pirates. But from that point, the Braves began a slow slide from prominence. In 1961 they were fourth. Then they finished fifth in 1962, sixth in 1963, and fifth in both 1964 and 1965.

Aaron, meanwhile, continued to put up seasons of excellence. In 1960, he led the NL with 126 RBIs. And in 1961 and 1962 he batted .327 and .323. Then, in 1963, he again came close to winning the Triple Crown. He led the league in home runs and RBIs, but he finished just seven

Four in a Row

On June 8, 1961, in the seventh inning of a game against the Reds at Cincinnati's Crosley Field, the Braves' Eddie Mathews hit a home run. Aaron followed with another. Then Joe Adcock and Frank Thomas hit back-to-back home runs. It was the first time in major league history that four players had hit consecutive home runs in a game.

points behind batting champion Tommy Davis of the
Los Angeles Dodgers. He also achieved a baseball rarity
by joining the so-called "30-30 Club" by stealing 30 or
more bases and hitting 30 or more home runs in the
same season.

Aaron's ability to hit, hit with power, drive in runs,
steal bases, and field his position year after year had
earned him a spot at the top of the baseball pedestal
by 1963, when he was 29. Aaron's manager that
year, Bobby Bragan, said Aaron was the best hitter in
baseball. St. Louis Cardinals catcher Tim McCarver said
there was just no way to get Aaron out consistently.
And *Los Angeles Times* columnist Jim Murray wrote at
the end of that 1963 season that Aaron was every bit

Brave Brothers

Henry Aaron was joined
by his brother Tommie on the
Milwaukee Braves in 1962.
Tommie, five years younger, made
his big-league debut in the season
opener on April 10, when he also
collected his first hit. The brothers
went on to play together for parts
of seven seasons in Milwaukee
and Atlanta, until 1971. While
Henry was a star, Tommie was a
utility player. Together, they hit
768 home runs. That is a major
league record for brothers, but
Tommie hit just 13 of them.
Though Henry was quiet and
reserved in public, Tommie was
outgoing. Tommie could make
Henry laugh the way no one else
could. "He was just so different
from Hank. Hank was so reserved,"
said Carolyn Aaron, Tommie's
wife. "He was so outgoing."[3] In
1984, Tommie died of leukemia at
age 45.

Henry Aaron, *left*, and brother Tommie Aaron pose during the Milwaukee Braves' spring training in 1962.

as good or better than the Giants' Willie Mays, a more flamboyant talent who many fans considered the best player in the major leagues.

"With Willie, the effort is there," wrote Murray. "You see it. You empathize with it. You strain when he strains, struggle when he struggles. Willie is a bit of a ham. With Henry Louis Aaron, it's as smooth and effortless as a swan gliding across a lake. He underplays like a British actor. Willie attacks the game. Aaron just gets it to cooperate with him."[4]

A New Era

The next two seasons, Aaron hit .328 and .318 for a team that was going nowhere in the standings. But the Braves were about to go somewhere else to play. After the team drew more than 2 million fans per season from 1954 to 1957, attendance gradually declined along with the team's performance. By 1962, attendance dipped below 1 million per year. Even before it attracted just 555,584 fans in 1965, the team announced it would move to Atlanta in 1966.

When the team played its final game in Milwaukee on September 22, 1965, just 12,577 fans came out to watch the Braves lose 7–6 to the Dodgers. When longtime teammates Eddie Mathews and Aaron both came up for their at-bats in the eighth and ninth innings, respectively, each was given a standing ovation by fans.

For Aaron and Matthews, the city of Milwaukee would always be special. "I'm not ordinarily a sentimental guy, but this really shook me up," said Mathews of the emotional farewell.[5]

Home Run Derby

In 1960, Aaron took part in a TV show called *Home Run Derby*. Each show featured a home run contest between two big-league players. Winners received a check for $2,000, and Aaron won the most money during that season. He collected $13,500 over seven appearances. While participating on the series, Aaron decided he would change his approach to hitting in games and try to swing for more home runs because home run hitters received more attention and more money.

Aaron goes up the wall to try to steal a home run during a 1965 game at County Stadium in Milwaukee.

CHAPTER 6

The Braves moved to Atlanta Stadium in 1966.

On to Atlanta

The first time Aaron took batting practice at Atlanta Stadium in 1966, he knew he was in for something new. The city's elevation of more than 1,000 feet (305 m), and warm temperatures, especially in summer, allow the ball to carry very well, much better than in Milwaukee.

"If you could get the ball into the air, there was a good chance that it wouldn't come down in the playing field," Aaron said after seeing his fly balls vanish over the outfield fence.[1] Aaron could see that if he concentrated on trying to pull the ball to left field, where the fence was closer, he might be able to hit more home runs in his new home.

More than 50,000 fans turned out on April 12 for the team's first game. The Braves hosted the Pittsburgh Pirates, and the excitement and atmosphere reminded Aaron of what it had been like in Milwaukee years before.

Atlanta mayor Ivan Allen Jr., who had led the campaign to bring baseball to Atlanta, threw out the ceremonial first pitch before the game. When Braves starting pitcher Tony Cloninger soon followed with his first pitch to Pirates leadoff hitter Matty Alou, major league baseball had officially come to the Deep South.

The Braves of 1966 had a strong lineup of hitters that also included third baseman Eddie Mathews, Aaron's longtime teammate, and outfielders Felipe Alou, Mack Jones, and Rico Carty, first baseman Lee Thomas, and catcher Joe Torre. But opening night ended in disappointment with a 3–2, 13-inning loss to Pittsburgh.

In their first season in Atlanta, the Braves finished fifth in the NL. But as Aaron had predicted, the team's new home proved to be a great place to hit. The Braves led the NL with 207 home runs. They outscored every team in the league. Plus their team .263 batting average was second in the league. The stadium quickly was nicknamed "The Launching Pad" for the way the ball flew out of the park.

No More Dynamic Duo

On December 31, 1966, the Braves traded Eddie Mathews to the Houston Astros. The move left Aaron shaken. Since breaking into the big leagues in 1954 in Milwaukee, Aaron had played with Mathews. Each had great respect for the other and had become good friends. Aaron would never forgive Paul Richards, the Braves' general manager, for making the trade or for the fact Mathews had to learn about it from a reporter.

Henry Aaron follows through on his swing during a June 1968 game against the Cincinnati Reds.

Aaron hit .279 in 1966. It was his lowest batting average since coming to the big leagues, but his 44 home runs and 127 RBIs were league bests and he was an All-Star for the twelfth straight season. He again led the NL in home runs in 1967 with 39, and he followed that up with 29 home runs in 1968.

Aaron hit his 500th career home run on July 14, 1968, becoming at 34 the second-youngest and eighth player overall to reach the milestone.

Back in the South

Though nothing, it seemed, could keep Aaron from continuing to blast the baseball, he found playing in Atlanta to be a big change. African Americans in the South still faced more racism than they did in the North, and many whites and white-owned businesses still weren't open to the idea of equal rights and equal access. Lester Maddox, a white man who was elected governor of Georgia in 1966, had been elected on a platform favoring segregation. That is a policy that legally required black people to use separate public facilities from white people. Blacks even had to use different drinking fountains than whites. Often, too,

Pro Sports in Atlanta

When the Braves moved to Atlanta for the 1966 season, it was a big step toward breaking racial barriers and old attitudes. The Braves, with several African-American players, including Aaron, became the South's first professional sports team. Soon came the National Football League's Falcons later in 1966 and the National Basketball Association's Hawks in 1968.

Atlanta Mayor Ivan Allen Jr. believed the addition of pro sports would help create a "New South" that would reject segregation. The new teams, in fact, were prohibited from creating separate seating areas for races. For the first time, whites and blacks in Atlanta could sit together and use the same facilities.

"Henry Aaron was a big part of that because he integrated pro sports in the Deep South, which was no small thing," said Jimmy Carter, a Georgian who would one day become president. "He was the first black man that white fans in the South cheered for."[2]

Aaron and his friends and family were subjected to racist comments at the ballpark and around town.

So Aaron, who often spoke his mind about equal rights, sometimes felt uncomfortable and wary in Atlanta. "As much as I wanted the city on my side, I just couldn't bring myself to be buddy-buddy with a crowd of white Southerners," he said.[3]

At that time, however, civil rights leaders in the South such as Martin Luther King Jr. and Andrew Young believed Aaron could make a strong, positive impact on race relations through his status as a baseball star. They told Aaron that by being a role model he could do great things. He would be the first black sports star in the South. When Aaron said he was embarrassed that he wasn't doing more for race relations, they assured him he was.

"We told him not to worry," Young said. "When you talked to Henry Aaron, you knew how he felt about civil rights. We told him just to keep hitting that ball. That was his job."[4]

Aaron did just that. And in 1969 the Braves' slugger, now 35, hit 44 home runs, drove in 97 runs, and hit .300 to help his team reach the postseason for

"For me, he was the toughest out. Everybody else, I had a plan. It may not work out, but I knew what I was going to try and do that day. But Henry, I just never, ever figured out what I was going to do."[5]
—*Los Angeles Dodgers Hall of Fame pitcher Sandy Koufax on what it was like to pitch to Aaron*

the first time since 1958. It was an expansion year in baseball. Two teams were added to both the NL and AL. So each league was split into two, six-team divisions for the first time. The Braves finished 93–69 to win the NL West by three games.

That set up a best-of-five NL Championship Series (NLCS) against the New York Mets, the surprise winners of the East. New York swept the series in three games, despite a magnificent performance by Aaron in what would be the last postseason experience of his career. Aaron hit a home run in each of the three games, batted .357, and drove in seven runs.

Aaron's hitting was even more remarkable considering he had badly cut his hand in an off-field accident just before the Mets series. He received some pain-killing shots, wore a protective glove, and went to work, impressing his teammates.

"From that day on, I said no man alive would ever compare with Hank Aaron," said young Braves outfielder Ralph Garr. "That was the thing that made me realize he wasn't like the rest of us."[6]

Miraculous, Indeed

The New York Mets team that beat the Braves in the 1969 NLCS wasn't expected to do anything before the season. Since joining the league in 1962, the Mets had finished last or next-to-last every season. But with great pitching, led by future Hall of Famer Tom Seaver, the "Miracle Mets" beat not only the Braves but also the favored Baltimore Orioles in the World Series.

Aaron, *left*, and Atlanta Braves manager Luman Harris watch a September 1969 game against the San Diego Padres.

CHAPTER 7

Henry Aaron records his 2,999th major league hit during a
May 1970 game against the Cincinnati Reds.

Making History

I t was the first inning of the second game of a doubleheader between the Braves and the Reds on May 17, 1970, when Aaron walked to home plate in Cincinnati. Aaron, 36, was off to a terrific start to his season, hitting .333 with 15 home runs in just 33 games.

The more than 33,000 fans at Crosley Field had turned out not only to see a game between two of the NL's top teams, but also to catch a bit of history. Aaron entered the day with 2,999 hits. With one more, he'd become just the ninth player in the more than 100-year history of baseball to reach 3,000. After going hitless in the first game, Aaron faced Reds 21-year-old rookie pitcher Wayne Simpson, who was just five when Aaron got his first hit in 1954.

Aaron hit a slow ground ball up the middle of the diamond and took off running. Before the Reds' infielder could pick it up and throw to first, Aaron had crossed the base. Hit number 3,000 was in the bag.

Former St. Louis Cardinals star Stan Musial, who was the only player still living at that time to have achieved 3,000 hits, jumped over a railing and ran to first base to congratulate Aaron, who then held up the ball and waved to the cheering crowd.

With the hit, Aaron also became the first player ever with 3,000 hits and 500 or more home runs, having entered the day with 569. Then, in his next at-bat, also against Simpson, Aaron crushed his 570th home run over the center-field fence. Though Aaron now was at an age when many players start to lose their skills, he clearly was still sharp.

After the game, Aaron was asked about not only his 3,000 hits, but the prospect of surpassing Babe Ruth's career home run record of 714.

"This year and the next are the critical ones for me if I am going to catch Ruth," he said. "I would almost have to have a 50 [home run] year in one of the two seasons. . . . Sure, catching Ruth would be a thrill, but achieving 3,000 hits is more remarkable because it shows consistency."[1]

Chasing History

If there was one thing Aaron always had been, it was consistent, and that didn't change even as he aged. He ended 1970 with 38 home runs. In 1971, he hit 47 more, including number 600 on April 27. That put him

Aaron hits his 600th career home run during an April 1971 game against the San Francisco Giants.

behind only Ruth and Willie Mays, who had 633 at the time. In 1972, Aaron hit 34 home runs, passing Mays to become number two all-time and give him 673 in his career. He was just 41 from tying Ruth's record. If everything came together in 1973, Aaron would become baseball's new home run champion.

But catching Ruth would not be just a numbers game. Once Aaron passed 600 home runs, the pressures on him began to mount as the media and fans now knew he had a good shot at the record. Circumstances outside baseball, too, were taking a toll.

Death of a Legend

The death of Jackie Robinson in 1972 made Aaron even more determined to become the home run champion. Robinson, who in 1947 had been an inspiration to a young Aaron and millions of other African Americans when he broke baseball's color barrier, had continued to speak out for racial equality. Aaron wanted to keep Robinson's dreams alive. "The best way I could do that was to become the all-time home run champion in the history of the game that had kept out black people for more than 60 years," he said.[3]

In 1971, Aaron's wife, Barbara, filed for divorce. Aaron moved out of their house and into an apartment in downtown Atlanta. He continued to stay involved with his four children, driving them to school and spending time with them. At the time, said Dusty Baker, Aaron's teammate and friend on the Braves, "Hank was as sad and lonesome as any man I ever saw."[2] Things began to get better in 1972, however. The Braves hired Aaron's friend and former longtime teammate Eddie

Aaron, *in black*, and Billye Williams, *right*, are married on
November 12, 1973, in Kingston, Jamaica.

Mathews to manage the team that year. Aaron also met
Atlanta television personality Billye Williams, whom he
soon began dating and married in 1973.

With the 1973 season about to begin, Aaron was
eager to have a great year and pass Ruth.

"Willie Mays was behind me, Mathews and Billye
were alongside, and Babe Ruth was straight ahead," he
said.[4] That positive attitude was soon wiped away.

Performing under Pressure

Aaron began receiving hate mail in small numbers in 1972. But then more and more arrived. As an African American playing in the 1950s and 1960s, Aaron always had encountered episodes of racism and threats. But as Aaron continued to hit home runs in 1973, people who didn't want to see Ruth's record broken by an African-American man wrote him hateful letters using racial slurs and death threats so vile that the FBI stepped in to monitor the mail and investigate threats. Said one letter writer: "Dear Hank Aaron, I got orders to do a bad job on you if and when you get 10 from B. Ruth record. A guy in Atlanta and a few in Miami, Fla, don't seem to care if they have to take care of your family, too."[5]

To be sure, the majority of mail received by Aaron was supportive. And the quantity of mail was enormous: an estimated 930,000 letters in 1973. As one fan wrote, "For years, sports fans have been waiting for the right man to come along and break that record. You, Henry Aaron, are

Public Support

Public support for Aaron became stronger in 1973 as news stories documented the hate mail he was receiving. Cartoonist Charles Schulz did his part to deride the bigots, using his nationally syndicated comic strip Peanuts to create a storyline in which his character, Snoopy the dog, was pursuing the home run record only to be swamped with hate mail from people who didn't consider him worthy. Said one character to Snoopy in one strip: "Hank Aaron is a great player . . . but you. If you break Babe Ruth's record, it'll be a disgrace. You're not even human!"[6]

that man."[7] Another, from a 12-year-old, said, "I have read many articles about the prejudice against you. I really think that's bad. I don't care what color you are. You could be green and it wouldn't matter."[8]

And, in cities all over the NL, Aaron mostly was cheered by fans who were appreciative of what he had done and was about to accomplish. But in Atlanta, crowds were often small, and random voices of racist fans were sometimes loud. To know that racism existed in the United States, and that he was hated simply for the color of his skin, made Aaron sad and angry. At one point he told his mother, "Mama, let them try to kill

Long Wait for 1974

As many as 300 reporters were following Aaron's every move by the end of the 1973 season. It was stressful for Aaron, who hated answering the same questions every day.

"I've reached the stage where I wish it was over and done with," he told the *Washington Post*. "I used to love to come to the ballpark. But now I hate it."[9]

When Aaron finished the 1973 season one home run short of Ruth's record, he told reporters he was afraid he might not be allowed to live to play in 1974 because of the death threats he had received. The sports editor of one Atlanta newspaper took the threats seriously enough to prepare an obituary for him. Aaron, however, tried to block it all out. If he could get a chance to bat in 1974, all the pressure and distractions would fade away.

"Pressure never bothered me at home plate," he said, "because nothing ever bothered me at home plate."[10]

me. That makes me more determined than ever to set that record."[11]

On July 21, Aaron hit home run number 700, and continued on a good pace. As he went into the final day of the season, he had hit 40 home runs and stood at 713. But in the final game, Aaron got three hits, all singles, and the record chase was put on hold.

Six months later, on 1974's Opening Day in Cincinnati, the 40-year-old Aaron tied the record with number 714 in his first at-bat of the new season. After sitting out the second game and going homerless in the third game, he headed back to Atlanta with a chance to break the record in the Braves' home opener. He didn't disappoint, with his record-breaking blast that put his chase to an end.

When the game was over, Mathews closed the doors to the locker room, climbed up on a table, and told his team what he thought about Aaron, whom he'd known and watched play for 20 years. He said Aaron was "the best ballplayer I ever saw in my life."[12] Then the team toasted Aaron with champagne.

Home for a Day

On August 6, 1973, Aaron had the chance to go home again. The Braves flew to Milwaukee to play an exhibition game against the Brewers, the AL team that had come to the city in 1970. It was billed as "Hank Aaron Day," and fans in Milwaukee gave their former baseball hero a warm welcome. More than 33,000 turned out for the game, which the Brewers won 7–5. Aaron received a standing ovation when he was introduced before the game. When he blasted a home run in the sixth inning, he received another long ovation.

Atlanta Braves teammates lift Aaron in celebration after Aaron hit his 715th career home run on April 8, 1974.

Henry Aaron waves to the crowd at Milwaukee County Stadium before his first home game with the Brewers in April 1975.

Back to Milwaukee

The 1974 season turned out to be the worst yet of Aaron's long career. As the season came to a close, many thought Aaron's baseball career would come to an end, too. But before he played the last game of that season, Aaron called a news conference to say he planned to play in 1975. It would not be with the Braves, however.

After 21 seasons, the relationship between Aaron and the organization had soured. In part it was because Aaron hoped to be offered a significant role as an executive with the team. Yet the Braves did not make an offer to Aaron's liking, and he didn't fit into their plans as a player, either. So Aaron asked for a trade.

It happened on November 2, 1974, when the Braves sent him to the AL's Milwaukee Brewers. It was a perfect situation for Aaron, who would be able to give his 41-year-old legs a rest in 1975 by serving as the team's designated hitter (DH). Only AL teams use the DH.

The Trade

When the Milwaukee Brewers traded for Aaron on November 2, 1974, they sent outfielder Dave May and pitcher Roger Alexander to the Atlanta Braves. May was the key player for the Braves. He had been an All-Star in 1973 while hitting .303 for the Brewers that season. He played two seasons in Atlanta in a career that lasted 12 years. However, the man who was traded for baseball's home run king hit just 96 home runs.

"I am thrilled to come back to the city where I started my baseball career, and I am happy that the Atlanta Braves saw fit to work so closely with me to meet my request," Aaron told reporters after learning of the trade.[1] The Braves wished Aaron luck, calling him the greatest Braves player of all time.

Brewers president Bud Selig was ecstatic to bring Aaron back to Milwaukee. "We are delighted to get a player who is unquestionably the greatest player of our generation," he said.[2]

More than 48,000 fans filled County Stadium to welcome back Hammerin' Hank for the Brewers' home opener on April 11. When he was introduced before the game and spoke to the crowd over the public-address system, he was loudly cheered. Then the fans serenaded him with a song to the tune of "Hello, Dolly":

Welcome home, Henry,
welcome home, Henry,
it's so nice to have you back
where you belong . . .[3]

Aaron, often characterized as unemotional, was touched by the moment. He told the fans he'd always have a special place in his heart for the people of Milwaukee.

In his first at-bat as the team's DH, Aaron walked. Later, he had a hit, scored a run, and drove in a run as Milwaukee beat the Cleveland Indians 6–2. All game, the crowd cheered his every move. After getting a hit in the sixth inning, Aaron said fans cheered as if he'd hit a home run.

Passing Ruth Again

Though Aaron was feeling his age, dealing with a bad back and leg problems, he was still a dangerous hitter and still breaking records. On May 1, in the Brewers' 17–3 victory over the visiting Detroit Tigers, Aaron went 4-for-4 and drove in two runs to set a major league record for career RBIs. His third-inning single drove in teammate Sixto Lezcano to give him 2,210 RBIs, breaking the mark of 2,209 held by Ruth. After all the fuss made over Aaron breaking Ruth's home run mark, the RBI record received little attention from the national media. This time, there wasn't a crowd of reporters following him.

"I've never set any plateaus," Aaron said after passing Ruth again. "I just try to do the best I can and

Fans at Milwaukee County Stadium hold a sign after Aaron recorded his 2,209th RBI, tying Babe Ruth, on May 1, 1975.

let the records fall. I just happened to be in the position to break one of the most historic records in baseball."[4]

In July, Aaron was selected to play in the All-Star Game for the twenty-first consecutive season, but his first as a member of the AL. He was hitting just .238 at the time with only nine home runs, but he was a sentimental pick as a reserve.

It would be his final All-Star appearance, and it would come at Milwaukee's County Stadium, the same home park in which he played his first All-Star Game in 1955. Aaron pinch hit in the second inning and lined out in his last All-Star at-bat.

Aaron finished the 1975 season hitting .234 with 12 home runs and 60 RBIs in 137 games. The Brewers finished fifth in the AL East. But Aaron's presence on the team had been a success with the fans. Attendance increased more than 250,000 from the previous season.

One Final Season

Aaron was disappointed in his performance and believed he could be better. He had one more year on his contract and vowed to improve in 1976. Yet at age 42 in 1976, Aaron soon discovered his skills were eroding. No longer was he Mr. Consistent. He wasn't even one of the top hitters on his team anymore.

"My eyes had deteriorated to the point where I needed glasses to read, my back still gave me trouble, and my knee

Designated Sitter

Though the DH rule allowed Aaron to play for the Brewers at ages 41 and 42, Aaron wasn't crazy about being a DH. After so many years playing in the field, Aaron said he found it hard to stay sharp while spending most of his time on the bench. "As a designated hitter, it was more difficult to keep my mind in the game. . . . I just didn't have the focus I'd always had before," he said.[5] In two seasons with the Brewers, he played just four games in the field.

was weak," he said. "I was like an old pitcher who can just throw his good fastball a few times every game."[6]

Still, he showed flashes of his old self. During an eight-game stretch in June, Aaron hit five home runs. Then in July, he hit a home run in the bottom of the 10th inning to give the Brewers a 5–4 victory over the Texas Rangers. The Milwaukee fans gave him a standing ovation. Knowing that the end of his career was near, Aaron savored the moment. "I knew I might never hear that again," he said.[7]

About a week later in a game against the California Angels on July 20, Aaron hit his tenth home run of the season. It was a line drive that landed in the left-field seats just inside the foul pole. It was the 755th home

Home Run No. 755

Because Aaron's final home run was hit in July 1976, not much thought was given to its significance. Two months remained in the season, and it was assumed Aaron would hit more. Aaron, in fact, didn't think much of it.

"I just don't remember the incident, who was on base or whether anyone was on base," Aaron said years later. "When you get to the end, you never know when this is going to be the last one."[8] The ball was picked up by Richard Arndt, a member of the County Stadium grounds crew. He kept it and sold it in 1999 for $650,000. While County Stadium is gone, the Brewers in 2007 put a plaque in the spot where the ball landed, which is now in a parking lot outside a Milwaukee youth baseball field.

run of his career. Though he didn't know it at the time, it would be his final home run.

As the season moved into September, Aaron announced he would retire at the end of the season. He had reached an agreement with Ted Turner, the young, new owner of the Atlanta Braves, to join the team as an executive. He was ready for new challenges.

On October 3, 1976, Aaron played his last major league game. In the bottom of the sixth inning of what would be a 5–2 loss to the Tigers, Aaron singled to knock in a run. As he stood on first base acknowledging the cheers, teammate Jim Gantner was sent out to pinch run for him. Aaron trotted into the dugout, waving to the fans.

Aaron left the field as baseball's all-time leader in home runs (755), RBIs (2,297), total bases (6,856), and

The Young and Old

When Aaron joined the Brewers in 1975, one teammate was shortstop Robin Yount, a 19-year-old in his second season. Yount was the youngest player in the big leagues. Aaron, 41, was the oldest. Yount was nervous and a bit scared to meet one of the game's biggest stars. Finally, Yount remembers finding his courage and walking up to Aaron and saying, "Hello, Mr. Aaron. I'm Robin Yount."[9] Yount would go on to play 20 big-league seasons, get more than 3,000 hits, and join Aaron in the Baseball Hall of Fame.

extra-base hits (1,477). His 21 seasons and 25 All-Star games remained a record in 2013. His 3,771 hits ranked second all-time when he retired. Plus, he was a model of consistency, retiring with a .305 career batting average.

But it was time to go. Henry Aaron couldn't play like Henry Aaron anymore.

"Wisconsin and the wonderful people there will always be special to me," Aaron said. "They treated me and my family so great. I'm so grateful I got to finish my career there. It was the only place I wanted to go."[10]

Aaron waves to fans during "Hank Aaron Night" at Milwaukee County Stadium late in the 1976 season.

CHAPTER 9

Atlanta Braves owner Ted Turner, *left*, introduces Henry Aaron to the press as a new team vice president.

After Baseball

Though Aaron had taken off his uniform and put away his bat, baseball's greatest slugger was determined to keep swinging for the fences. He had achieved fame by breaking Babe Ruth's home run record. Now he was determined to use his star status to work for racial equality.

Aaron moved back to Atlanta in late 1976 to become a vice president with the Braves in charge of the team's minor league system and player development. That made him one of the highest-ranking African-American executives in the major leagues. He planned to prove to baseball and the business world that he could be a difference-maker in the sport and in society. He would keep Jackie Robinson's legacy alive with his deeds.

"The way I see it, it's a great thing to be the man who hit the most home runs, but it's a greater thing to be the man who did the most with the home runs he hit," Aaron said. "So long as there's a chance that maybe I can hammer out a little justice now and then, or a little opportunity here and there, I intend to do as I always have: keep swinging."[1] Aaron believed he could use the home run record to break down walls that existed for African Americans in baseball, the business world, and education.

Many of those barriers had fallen since 1947 when Robinson broke into the big leagues, but some remained. Frank Robinson was hired as the major leagues' first African-American manager in 1975 with the Cleveland Indians, and Aaron became one of two high-ranking black executives in the big leagues the next year. But those numbers were tiny.

As far as Aaron was concerned, there was more work to be done. He was determined to campaign for

Pain Still Lingers

Decades after Aaron broke Babe Ruth's home run record, Aaron still carries the sting of the racist letters he received and the fear he felt from death threats. He's been a success in his business life and with his causes, takes great joy from his family, and has received countless honors. Yet he relishes his privacy and stays out of the public eye as much as possible and remains wary of strangers and crowds.

"Even now, assassination is always in the back of his mind," said Atlanta police officer Calvin Wardlaw, who was Aaron's bodyguard during the 1973 and 1974 seasons. "There's always the possibility someone will try to make a name at this late date."[2]

Aaron later said so many bad things happened during his chase for the record that there were things he was still trying to get over.

minority opportunity. He said there was no excuse that African Americans were underrepresented as managers and executives.

As Aaron took over his new position with the Braves under team owner Ted Turner, he embarked on a diverse post-playing career that included work in baseball, business, and public service. In 1980, he was promoted to senior vice president with the Braves.

Eventually, he was asked by MLB to establish programs to aid in the recruitment of minorities to the game and to leadership positions. Along the way, too, Aaron became the unofficial spokesman for baseball on minority issues, a role he found exciting after his early years in the game when African Americans were discouraged from speaking their minds.

"I don't think that baseball has done enough for minorities," Aaron said. "I speak out and talk about it simply because it's wrong. It's wrong for baseball to take black baseball players, put them on the field and after 10 years or so say, 'See you later.' But they don't treat white players like that. They give them opportunities. . . . It would be wrong for me to sit back and not voice my opinion about it."[3]

Influential Work

Outside of baseball, Aaron became a member of the board of directors of Turner Broadcasting System, and

A Well-Named Award

In 1999, in honor of Aaron's sixty-fifth birthday and the twenty-fifth anniversary of his home run record, MLB announced the creation of the Hank Aaron Award. It is given annually to the best hitter in the AL and NL, as voted on by a combination of fans and Hall of Famers. During the World Series each year since, Aaron has taken part in the presentation of the award.

established his own businesses, opening restaurants and car dealerships. He worked with the National Association for the Advancement of Colored People (NAACP) and the Boys and Girls Clubs of America. He and his wife, Billye, also started the Hank Aaron Chasing the Dream Foundation, a nonprofit dedicated to raising funds to create opportunities for young people from disadvantaged backgrounds. Also, in 1991, he published his autobiography, *I Had a Hammer: The Hank Aaron Story*, which became a best-selling book.

Though Aaron often felt overlooked when he was a player, he saw that perception change as he moved further from his playing days. The quiet man who had performed in cities far from the media spotlight began receiving his due.

Aaron, *left,* and fellow slugger Frank Robinson pose during the 1982 Baseball Hall of Fame ceremony in which both were inducted.

On August 1, 1982, he was inducted into the Baseball Hall of Fame, having been selected on 97.8 percent of ballots. That was the second-highest percentage ever to that point. It was a higher percentage than Willie Mays, Mickey Mantle, Stan Musial, or Sandy Koufax received. Higher even than Ruth.

"I took the talent that God gave me and tried to develop it to the best of my ability," Aaron said in his acceptance speech at the National Baseball Hall of Fame

Hall of Fame Plaque

All players enshrined at the National Baseball Hall of Fame and Museum in Cooperstown, New York, have a plaque describing their careers. Hank Aaron's plaque reads: "Hit 755 home runs in 23-year career to become majors' all-time homer king. Had 20 or more for 20 consecutive years, at least 30 in 15 seasons and 40 or better eight times. Also set records for games played (3,298), at-bats (12,364), long hits (1,477), total bases (6,856), runs batted in (2,297). Paced NL in batting twice and homers, runs batted in, and slugging pct. four times each. Won Most Valuable Player Award in NL in 1957."[6]

in Cooperstown, New York. "But I never dreamed then [as a rookie] that I would be in the Hall of Fame."[4]

Aaron added that he felt a sense of humility and gratitude to be inducted in the same location where black pioneers Jackie Robinson and Roy Campanella had previously stood after opening doors to the major leagues for others. "Man's ability is limited only by his lack of opportunity," Aaron said.[5]

Twenty years later, Aaron received the Presidential Medal of Freedom, the nation's highest civilian award, from President George W. Bush at a White House ceremony on July 9, 2002. It came about a year and a half after President Bill Clinton had presented Aaron with the Presidential Citizens Medal.

"Hank Aaron overcame poverty and racism to become one of the most accomplished baseball players of all time," said President Bush in the Presidential Medal of Freedom ceremony. "By steadily pursuing his calling in the face of unreasoning hatred, Hank Aaron has proven himself a great human being as well as a great athlete."[7]

In addition, Aaron's name and likeness are scattered across the country in his honor. The baseball stadium in his hometown of Mobile, Alabama, is named Hank Aaron Stadium. Statues of Aaron stand outside the Brewers' Miller Park in Milwaukee and Braves' Turner Field in Atlanta, as well as the minor league Carson Park in Eau Claire, Wisconsin, the city where Aaron first played as a minor leaguer. Both the Braves and Brewers have retired his No. 44.

In the decades since he retired as a player, Aaron has done what he set out to do,

A Hitter's Park

In 1996, there was a push in Atlanta to name the Braves' new baseball stadium for Aaron. The drive failed, however, and it was instead named Turner Field in honor of team owner Ted Turner. However, the street outside the stadium bears Aaron's name, and the ballpark address reflects his home run total: 755 Hank Aaron Drive.

open doors for others. In the twenty-first century, more African Americans have become managers and executives in baseball, and thousands of young people have been helped along in life by Aaron's good works. He says he feels obligated to speak up and help out.

"I can't let Jackie [Robinson] down, or my people, or myself," he said. "The day I become content is the day I cease to be anything more than a man who hit home runs."[8]

Aaron holds up an Atlanta Braves jersey after the team retired his No. 44 in 1977. His wife Billye looks on.

San Francisco Giants slugger Barry Bonds celebrates after hitting his 756th career home run on August 7, 2007.

His Place in History

San Francisco Giants star Barry Bonds stood at home plate watching the flight of the baseball he had just struck. As the ball soared on a long, high arc toward the seats beyond the fence in right-center field, Bonds thrust both arms into the air in triumph.

On August 7, 2007, Bonds's quest was complete. As the ball settled into a mass of fans, Bonds became baseball's new home run king. Thirty-three years after Henry Aaron passed Babe Ruth to become the game's number-one slugger, Bonds passed Aaron. Thirty-one years after Aaron hit the 755th and final home run of his long career, Bonds hit his 756th into the cool air of San Francisco's AT&T Park.

As Bonds made his slow trot around the bases, Giants fans cheered, fireworks exploded and the enormous ballpark video board flashed the message, "Road to History: Bonds 756." After crossing home plate, Bonds was greeted by his son, Nikolai, a Giants bat boy, who held up one finger to signal that his dad was number one. A few moments later, Aaron appeared on the video board to congratulate Bonds. In a messaged taped approximately one month earlier, Aaron said:

> I would like to offer my congratulations to Barry Bonds on becoming baseball's career home run leader. It is a great accomplishment which required skill, longevity, and determination. Throughout the past century, the home run has held a special place in baseball, and I have been privileged to hold this record for 33 of those years. I move over now and offer my best wishes to Barry and his family on this historic achievement.
>
> My hope today, as it was on that April evening in 1974, is that the achievement of this record will inspire others to chase their own dreams.[1]

After the game, Bonds said Aaron's message was important to him. A Giants executive added that Aaron's words were important not only for Bonds, but to help create some closure for people. After all, Bonds's chase of Aaron's record created controversy.

Aaron-Bonds Connection

When Aaron hit the 755th and final home run of his career in 1976 against the California Angels, the Angels' right fielder in that game was Bobby Bonds. Thirty-one years later, Bobby's son, Barry, hit his 756th home run to break Aaron's record. With Barry that night at the game was Willie Mays, his godfather. Mays and Aaron played 21 seasons against each other in the NL.

Bonds was one of the finest players of his time, but baseball in the 1990s and 2000s was labeled the "steroid era" because of the widespread use of performance-enhancing drugs such as steroids and human growth hormone. During this period, numbers of home runs increased dramatically, in part because already skilled hitters were increasing muscle mass and bat speed.

During this period, players hit 50 or more home runs in a season 25 times, compared with just four such seasons from 1960 to 1990. In 1998, Mark McGwire hit 70 home runs and Sammy Sosa hit 66 to break the single-season record of 61 set by Roger Maris in 1961. Just three seasons later, Bonds hit 73 home runs to break McGwire's mark.

After that record season of 2001, Bonds continued to hit home runs in bunches, inching ever closer to Aaron's record. But as Bonds's home run total increased, so did the number of his critics. Though Bonds had not tested positive for banned substances at the time, he had been the subject of a major league investigation because of allegations he used them. Many baseball followers assumed he was guilty, lumping him in with players who had failed drug tests or admitted use. They resented his assault on Aaron's record.

Often, fans in opposing ballparks chanted "ster-roids" or booed when Bonds came to the plate and held up signs that called him a cheater. In San Diego in 2006, a fan even threw a syringe toward Bonds in left field, insinuating he used drugs.

Appreciation for Aaron

Throughout Bonds's quest to break his record, Aaron remained mostly quiet. He refused to be pulled into conversations about the steroid era and would not answer questions about Bonds or the possibility that Bonds used banned substances. And as Bonds climbed within a few home runs of the record, Aaron declined Bonds's invitations to speak with him or to travel to games to be present for home run number 756. When Aaron learned Bonds was hurt by his decision to keep his distance, he still didn't budge.

"I'm sorry Barry feels that way, and I don't have any resentment toward him whatsoever, but I have no intention of trying to get in contact with him or doing anything with him in regard to his [chasing the record]," Aaron said. "Nothing. Why should I? It's really not a big concern of mine. I don't know why I should have to do anything. I might

"Slapping a rattlesnake across the face with the back of your hand is safer than trying to fool Henry Aaron."[2]
—*Pitcher Claude Osteen on how difficult it was to get Aaron out*

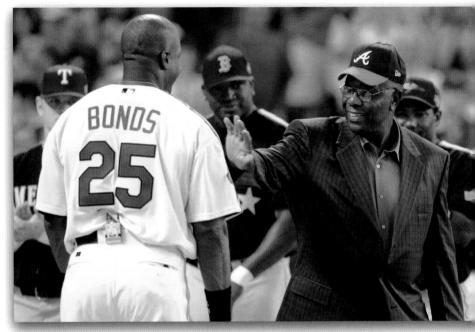

Henry Aaron, *right*, greets Barry Bonds before the 2004 All-Star Home Run Derby.

send him a telegram and that would be the extent of it. . . . I'm 72 years old and I'm not hopping on a plane and flying all the way to San Francisco for anybody."[3]

In a roundabout way, Bonds's chase of Aaron's record shined a new light on the long-retired star. As the nation focused on Bonds's mounting home run total, the media and former players revisited the greatness of Aaron. Fans too young to have watched him play saw his highlight films and read about his accomplishments. Older fans turned off by the steroid era and by Bonds in particular looked back and recalled the way Aaron played with grace, professionalism, and dignity even in the face of enormous pressures during his own home run chase.

Long after his career, Aaron finally seemed to garner a wide appreciation from the public that had often eluded him as a player. Weeks before Bonds hit his 756th home run, Hall of Fame slugger Reggie Jackson said he expected that Bonds would break the record, but said he wouldn't eclipse it. Aaron, he said, would be "the people's home run king."[4] *Sports Illustrated* columnist Rick Reilly had a similar view, writing: "Just because a thief paints over a masterpiece doesn't mean the masterpiece isn't still underneath."[5] Another Hall of Fame hitter, Harmon Killebrew, said that as far as he was concerned, Aaron would still be the home run champ.

A Place in History

Though Bonds passed him, Aaron holds an honored place in the game. More than 30 years after his final game, in 2013, he ranked number one all-time in total bases and RBIs. He was second in home runs and at-bats, third in hits and games played, and fourth in runs scored. He won three Gold Gloves for fielding excellence, held two batting titles, and was an excellent base runner, successful on 77 percent of his stolen-base attempts.

It was never his goal as a baseball player to be the sport's all-time home run king, he said. He simply wanted to be the best all-around player he could be. In fact, he said his record for total bases is more representative of "what I was all about as a hitter."[6] Plus, said his contemporaries, he did it all in an understated, dignified manner. Baseball commissioner Bud Selig, a longtime friend, said, "Hank Aaron is one of the most principled persons you will ever know."[7]

Two years after Bonds broke his record, Aaron stayed on that principled path. When many baseball writers and former players argued that players such

Hall of Fame Display

In April 2009, the Baseball Hall of Fame in Cooperstown, New York, opened a permanent exhibit called "Hank Aaron: Chasing the Dream." The exhibit chronicles Aaron's life and career and documents his achievements with photos, stories, and artifacts. Aaron attended the opening of the exhibit and thanked the people who helped make his life and career special.

"No matter what you accomplish, what you achieve, you don't go down the path by yourself," he said.[8] Jeff Idelson, president of the National Baseball Hall of Fame and Museum, said the "Chasing the Dream" exhibit allows fans to "learn about a man who was a Hall of Famer in every sense."[9]

Among the items on display are Aaron's 1957 World Series ring, his MVP Award, the uniform he wore while hitting his 715th home run, and the bats and balls from his 3,000th hit and 500th and 600th home runs.

Advocate for Asterisks

Aaron has said that players who use banned substances should not be banned from the Hall of Fame. But in 2009, he said that if players known to have used steroids are elected, they should have an asterisk on their plaque with an acknowledgement they used performance-enhancing drugs. "To be safe, that's the only way I see you can do it," he said. "I played the game long enough to know it is impossible for players, I don't care who it is, to hit 70-plus home runs [in a season]. It just does not happen."[12]

as Bonds and McGwire should have their records erased, Aaron disagreed.

"In all fairness to everybody, I just don't see how you really can do a thing like that and just say somebody isn't the record-holder anymore, and let's go back to the way that it was," he said. "If you did that, you'd have to go back and change all kinds of records, and the [home run] record was very important to me. It's probably the most hallowed record out there. . . . But now it's in the hands of somebody else."[10]

To those who saw him play, Aaron always will be special, record or no record. Hammerin' Hank was one of a kind.

"Henry was as pure as there was," said Phil Niekro, a longtime Braves teammate and Hall of Fame pitcher. "I think the words 'pure' and 'clean' are the best words to describe how he played. Henry just played the game the way it was meant to be played. He wasn't looking for the spotlight. There were no smoking guns surrounding him. He made the game look simple."[11]

Aaron is remembered for playing the game the right way.

1934

Henry Louis Aaron is born on February 5 in Mobile, Alabama.

1951

Aaron signs with the Indianapolis Clowns of the Negro American League on November 20.

1952

On June 14, Aaron signs with the Boston Braves, who assign him to play for their minor league team in Eau Claire, Wisconsin.

1954

Aaron hits his first home run in the major leagues on April 23, also against the Cardinals.

1954

Aaron finishes fourth in the NL Rookie of the Year voting. He becomes a father with the birth of his daughter, Gaile.

1955

Aaron is selected to play in his first All-Star Game.

1953

Aaron is promoted to the Braves' minor league team in Jacksonville, Florida. He is selected as league MVP and also marries Barbara Lucas.

1954

Aaron makes his major league debut for the Milwaukee Braves on April 13 against the Cincinnati Reds, going 0-for-5.

1954

Aaron gets his first major league hit on April 15 against the St. Louis Cardinals.

1956

Aaron wins the NL batting championship with a .328 average.

1957

Aaron leads the NL in home runs and RBIs and is NL MVP. The Braves win the NL pennant and beat the New York Yankees in the World Series.

1958

Aaron hits .326 to help the Braves win a second straight NL title. Milwaukee loses to the Yankees in a World Series rematch.

1959

Aaron hits .355, the best average of his career, to win a second NL batting championship.

1963

Aaron joins the "30-30 Club" by hitting 30 or more home runs with 30 or more stolen bases in one season. He has 44 home runs and 31 stolen bases.

1968

On July 14, Aaron becomes the eighth player to hit 500 home runs.

1974

Aaron hits home run number 715 on April 8, passing Babe Ruth to become baseball's all-time home run leader.

1974

The Braves trade Aaron to the Milwaukee Brewers on November 2.

1975

Aaron drives in his 2,210th run on May 1 to pass Ruth to become baseball's all-time leader in RBIs.

1970

Aaron gets his 3,000th career hit on May 17 against the Cincinnati Reds.

1971

Aaron hits his 600th career home run on April 27.

1973

Aaron hits his 700th career home run on July 21. He marries Billye Williams on November 13.

1976

Aaron hits the final home run of his career, number 755, against the California Angels on July 20.

1982

Aaron is inducted into the National Baseball Hall of Fame on August 1.

2002

Aaron receives the Presidential Medal of Freedom, the nation's highest civilian award, at the White House on July 9.

DATE OF BIRTH

February 5, 1934

PLACE OF BIRTH

Mobile, Alabama

PARENTS

Herbert and Estella Aaron

EDUCATION

Central High School and Josephine Allen Institute in Mobile, Alabama

MARRIAGES

Barbara Lucas, 1953 (divorced 1971)

Billye Williams, 1973

CHILDREN

Gaile (1954), Henry Jr. (1957), twins Lary and Gary (1957; Gary died as an infant), Dorinda (1962), and Ceci (adopted, daughter of Billye Williams).

CAREER HIGHLIGHTS

Aaron played 23 seasons in the major leagues and was elected to the National Baseball Hall of Fame in 1982. He has more RBIs and total bases than any player in history and ranks second in home runs and third in hits through 2013.

SOCIAL CONTRIBUTIONS

Aaron has worked to provide equal opportunities for minorities in sports and in society while contributing to multiple organizations that provide aid to people in need. He and his wife, Billye, created a foundation to help young people get educational and career opportunities.

CONFLICTS

In his second season of professional baseball, Aaron became one of the first African-American players to play in the South Atlantic League. Because of his race, he was forced to stay and eat in separate hotels and restaurants from his white teammates and was subjected to racist taunts. Aaron again felt the sting of racism after the Braves moved to Atlanta. Fans sent him death threats as he closed in on Babe Ruth's all-time home run record.

QUOTE

"I've been misunderstood by a lot of people, simply because I don't talk a lot. And when I do talk, people think that I'm an angry person. I'm not an angry person, because I feel an angry person is not a successful person." —*Henry Aaron*

GLOSSARY

amateur

An athlete not allowed to be paid for competing.

bigots

People who are intolerant.

color barrier

The term used to describe how organized baseball kept African-American players from playing with white players.

commissioner

The chief executive.

contract

A legal agreement that defines a player's terms of service, such as length committed to a team and salary.

designated hitter (DH)

A position used by baseball's AL since 1973 that replaces the pitcher in a team's batting lineup. The designated hitter does not play in the field.

exhibition

A game that does not count in the standings. None of the statistics from these games count toward a player's career record.

expansion

Adding something new, such as teams to a league. Brand new teams are called expansion teams.

obituary

An announcement of somebody's death.

pennant

A long, triangular flag. In baseball, the word is used to describe a league championship.

promoted

When a player is moved to a better league.

retire

To end something, such as a career. In baseball, teams sometimes retire jersey numbers of legendary players so that future players can never wear the same number.

rookie

A first-year player in the major leagues.

segregation

The system especially prevalent in the South that kept whites and African Americans from sharing the same facilities, schools, and sports leagues.

semipro

Being paid for a job but not enough to be considered full-time.

total bases

The number of bases a player advances on his hits.

utility player

A baseball player who can play several defensive positions.

ADDITIONAL RESOURCES

SELECTED BIBLIOGRAPHY

Aaron, Hank, with Lonnie Wheeler. *I Had a Hammer: The Hank Aaron Story*. New York: Harper Perennial, 1991.

Bryant, Howard. *The Last Hero: A Life of Henry Aaron*. New York: Pantheon Books, 2010.

Moffi, Larry, and Jonathan Kronstadt. *Crossing the Line: Black Major Leaguers, 1947–59*. Jefferson, NC: McFarland & Company, Inc., 1994.

Rains, Rob. *Rawlings Presents Big Stix: Greatest Hitters in the History of the Major Leagues*. Champaign, IL: Sports Publishing LLC, 2004.

Stanton, Tom. *Hank Aaron and the Home Run That Changed America*. New York: Harper Perennial, 2005.

FURTHER READINGS

Creamer, Robert. *Babe: The Legend Comes to Life*. New York: Simon & Schuster, 1992.

Herman, Bruce. *Hall of Fame Players: Cooperstown*. Lincolnwood, IL: Publications International, 2007.

Hogan, Lawrence D. *Shades of Glory: The Negro Leagues & the Story of African-American Baseball*. Washington DC: National Geographic Society, 2006.

Poling, Jerry. *A Summer Up North: Henry Aaron and the Legend of Eau Claire Baseball*. Madison, WI: University of Wisconsin Press, 2002.

Wilkinson, Jack. *Game of my Life: Atlanta Braves*. Champaign, IL: Sports Publishing LLC, 2007.

WEB LINKS

To learn more about Hank Aaron, visit ABDO Publishing Company online at **www.abdopublishing.com**. Web sites about Hank Aaron are featured on our Book Links page. These links are routinely monitored and updated to provide the most current information available.

PLACES TO VISIT

Hank Aaron Stadium
755 Bolling Brothers Boulevard, Mobile, AL 36606.
251-479-2327
www.milb.com/content/page.jsp?sid=t417&ymd=20090310&content_id=522110&vkey=team1
The home of the Mobile Bay Bears minor league team includes the Hank Aaron Museum at the park. Aaron's childhood home, moved to the site of the park, is part of the museum.

National Baseball Hall of Fame and Museum
25 Main Street, Cooperstown, NY 13326
888-425-5633
www.baseballhall.org
The official Hall of Fame of professional baseball features 50,000 square feet of exhibit space over three floors. Exhibits include plaques of every person selected to the Hall of Fame, artifacts, and movies.

Turner Field
755 Hank Aaron Drive, Atlanta, GA 30315
404-614-2310
braves.mlb.com/atl/ballpark
The ballpark of the Atlanta Braves includes the Ivan Allen Jr. Braves Museum & Hall of Fame, with more than 600 Braves artifacts and photographs.

CHAPTER 1. The New King

1. Lee Jenkins. "Legendary Voice Will Let Fans Do Call on Bonds." *New York Times*. The New York Times Co., 1 Aug. 2007. Web. 6 May 2013.
2. Jim Murray. "Henry Aaron Finds a Niche All His Own." *Los Angeles Times*. The Tribune Co., 8 Feb. 1987. Web. 6 May 2013.
3. Ron Fimrite. "End of the Glorious Ordeal." *SI Vault*. Time, Inc., 15 April 1974. Web. 6 May 2013.
4. Ibid.
5. Mike Capuzzo. "Prisoner of Memory." *SI Vault*. Time, Inc., 7 Dec. 1992. Web. 6 May 2013.
6. Larry Schwartz. "Hank Aaron: Hammerin' Back at Racism," *ESPN.com*. The Walt Disney Co., 1999. Web. 6 May 2013.
7. "Aaron Didn't Enjoy Record Bid." *Los Angeles Times*. The Tribune Co., 26 Aug. 1987. Web. 6 May 2013.
8. Matt Crossman. "Catching Aaron's 715th HR: Tom House Recalls How He Reached the HOF." *The Sporting News*. Perform Sporting News Limited, 8 April 2011. Web. 6 May 2013.
9. "Aaron Leaves Ruth's Ghost Behind, Can Relax." *The Geneva Times*. The Associated Press, 8 April 1974. Web. 6 May 2013.

CHAPTER 2. Humble Beginnings

1. Tom Stanton. *Hank Aaron and the Home Run that changed America*. New York: It Books, 2005. Web. 6 May 2013.
2. Charlie Vascellaro. *Hank Aaron: A Biography*. Westport, CT: Greenwood, 2005. Web. 11 May 2013.
3. Larry Moffi and Jonathan Kronstadt. *Crossing the Line: Black Major Leaguers, 1947–1959*. Jefferson, NC: McFarland & Company, Inc., 1994. Web. 10 May 2013.
4. Ibid.

CHAPTER 3. Welcome to the Big Leagues

1. Hank Aaron with Lonnie Wheeler. *I Had a Hammer: The Hank Aaron Story*. New York: Harper Perennial, 1991. Print. 119.
2. Ibid. 120.
3. "Aaron, Hank." *Baseballhall.org*. Baseball Hall of Fame and Museum, 1982. Web. 12 May 2013.
4. Lou Chapman. "Confident Braves Break Spring Camp." *Milwaukee Sentinel*. Journal Communications, 25 March 1955. Web. 12 May 2003.
5. "19-year-old Gaile Aaron Talks about Her Dad Hank." *The Afro-American*. Afro-American Newspapers, 29 Sept. 1973. Web. 13 May 2013.
6. Hank Aaron with Lonnie Wheeler. *I Had a Hammer: The Hank Aaron Story*. New York: Harper Perennial, 1991. Print. 126.

7. Jim Rednour. "500 HRC Members Cheered Each Other On." *500 Home Run Club*. 500 Home Run Club, LLC., 1 Oct. 2012. Web. 12 May 2013.

CHAPTER 4. Champions

1. Roy Terrell. "Murder with A Blunt Instrument." *SI Vault*. Time, Inc., 12 Aug. 1957. Web. 13 May 2013.

2. Ibid.

3. Ibid.

4. Ibid.

5. Gary D'Amato. "Aaron did it all for '57 Braves." *Milwaukee Journal Sentinel*. Journal Communications, 26 Feb. 2012. Web. 13 May 2013.

6. Hank Aaron with Lonnie Wheeler. *I Had a Hammer: The Hank Aaron Story*. New York: Harper Perennial, 1991. Print. 178.

7. Ibid. 187.

8. Ibid. 182.

CHAPTER 5. Taking His Place

1. Hank Aaron with Lonnie Wheeler. *I Had a Hammer: The Hank Aaron Story*. New York: Harper Perennial, 1991. Print. 191.

2. Ibid. 197.

3. Howard Bryant. *The Last Hero: A Life of Henry Aaron*. New York: Pantheon Books, 2010. Web. 14 May 2013.

4. Bruce Jenkins. "Who's Worse? Nobody." *San Francisco Chronicle*. Hearst Corp., 12 Aug. 2007. Web. 13 May 2013.

5. Bill Chuck and Jim Kaplan. *Walkoffs, Last Licks and Final Outs: Baseball's Grand (and Not-So-Grand) Finales*. Chicago, IL: ACTA Sports, 2008. Web. 14 May 2013.

CHAPTER 6. On to Atlanta

1. Hank Aaron with Lonnie Wheeler. *I Had a Hammer: The Hank Aaron Story*. New York: Harper Perennial, 1991. Print. 248.

2. Howard Bryant. "Atlanta Pro Sports and Integration." *SI Vault*. Time, Inc., 12 Jan. 2011. Web. 16 May 2013.

3. Hank Aaron with Lonnie Wheeler. *I Had a Hammer: The Hank Aaron Story*. New York: Harper Perennial, 1991. Print. 254.

4. Howard Bryant. "Atlanta Pro Sports and Integration." *SI Vault*. Time, Inc., 12 Jan. 2011. Web. 16 May 2013.

5. Larry Schwartz. "Hank Aaron: Hammerin' Back at Racism." *ESPN.com*. The Walt Disney Co., 1999. Web. 6 May 2013.

6. Hank Aaron with Lonnie Wheeler. *I Had a Hammer: The Hank Aaron Story*. New York: Harper Perennial, 1991. Print. 278.

CHAPTER 7. Making History

1. William Leggett. "Henry Raps One For History." *SI Vault*. Time, Inc., 25 May 1970. Web. 12 May 2013.

2. Hank Aaron with Lonnie Wheeler. *I Had a Hammer: The Hank Aaron Story*. New York: Harper Perennial, 1991. Print. 292.

3. Ibid. 309.

4. Ibid. 314.

5. Mike Capuzzo. "Prisoner of Memory." *SI Vault*, Time, Inc., 7 Dec. 1992. Web. 6 May 2013.

6. Jim Caple. "Aaron's reign: 20 years and counting." *Boca-Raton News*. Knight-Ridder Newspapers, 8 April 1994. Web. 18 May 2013.

7. Hank Aaron with Lonnie Wheeler. *I Had a Hammer: The Hank Aaron Story*. New York: Harper Perennial, 1991. Print. 332.

8. Ibid. 332.

9. Charlie Vascellaro. *Hank Aaron: A Biography*. Westport, CT.: Greenwood, 2005. Web. 11 May 2013.

10. Hank Aaron with Lonnie Wheeler. *I Had a Hammer: The Hank Aaron Story*. New York: Harper Perennial, 1991. Print. 357.

11. Mike Capuzzo. "Prisoner of Memory." *SI Vault*. Time, Inc., 7 Dec. 1992. Web. 6 May 2013.

12. Hank Aaron with Lonnie Wheeler. *I Had a Hammer: The Hank Aaron Story*. New York: Harper Perennial, 1991. Print. 372.

CHAPTER 8. Back to Milwaukee

1. "Henry Aaron Traded to Brewers." *Tri Cities Daily*. The Associated Press. The Associated Press, 3 Nov. 1974. Web. 20 May 2013.

2. Ibid.

3. Larry Keith. "Back Where He Belongs." *SI Vault*. Time, Inc., 21 April 1975. Web. 22 May 2013.

4. Ken Rappoport. "Aaron Breaks Another Ruth Record." *The Citizen-Advertiser*. The Associated Press, 2 May 1975. Web. 22 May 2013.

5. Hank Aaron with Lonnie Wheeler. *I Had a Hammer: The Hank Aaron Story*. New York: Harper Perennial, 1991. Print. 407.

6. Ibid. 408.

7. Ibid. 409.

8. Kelvin Ang. "Brewers Pinpoint Aaron's Final Homer." *MLB.com*. Major League Baseball, 7 June 2007. Web. 23 May 2013.

9. Steve Wulf. "Robin Yount." *SI Vault*. Time, Inc., 21 Feb. 1994. Web. 23 May 2013.

10. Bob Nightengale. "Hammerin' Hank Had Weary Finish to Milwaukee Career." *USA Today*. Gannett Co. 20 June 2007. Web. 23 May 2013.

CHAPTER 9. After Baseball

1. Hank Aaron with Lonnie Wheeler. *I Had a Hammer: The Hank Aaron Story*. New York: Harper Perennial, 1991. Print. 6.

2. Mike Capuzzo. "Prisoner of Memory." *SI Vault*. Time, Inc., 7 Dec. 1992. Web. 6 May 2013.

3. "A Candid Talk with a Legend." *TBS.com*. Turner Broadcasting System, Inc., 1996. Web. 24 May 2013.

4. "Frank & Hank Join Hall of Fame." *Daytona Beach Sunday News-Journal*. The Associated Press, 2 Aug. 1982. Web. 24 May 2013.

5. Ibid.

6. "Aaron, Hank." *Baseballhall.org*. Baseball Hall of Fame and Museum, 1982. Web. 12 May 2013.

7. "Bill Cosby, Hank Aaron and Nelson Mandela Receive Presidential Medal of Freedom." *Jet Magazine*. Johnson Publishing Co., 29 July 2002. Web. 26 May 2013.

8. "A Candid Talk with a Legend." *TBS.com*. Turner Broadcasting System, Inc., 1996. Web. 24 May 2013.

CHAPTER 10. His Place in History

1. "Hank Aaron Statement on Barry Bonds' Achievement." *USA Today*. The Associated Press, 8 Aug. 2007. Web. 25 May 2013.

2. Rob Rains. *Rawlings Presents Big Stix: Greatest Hitters in the History of the Major Leagues*. Champaign, IL: Sports Publishing LLC, 2004. Print. 4.

3. Michael Hunt. "Aaron Is Right to Avoid Bonds Circus." *Milwaukee Journal Sentinel*. Journal Communications, 22 April 2007. Web. 24 May 2013.

4. Tom Verducci. "The People's King." *SI Vault*. Time, Inc., 23 July 2007. Web. 25 May 2013.

5. Rick Reilly. "Giving Barry His Due." *SI Vault*. Time, Inc., 23 July 2007. Web. 25 May 2013.

6. Tom Verducci. "The People's King." *SI Vault*. Time, Inc., 23 July 2007. Web. 25 May 2013.

7. Ibid.

8. Samantha Carr. "Hank Aaron Thrills Overflow Crowd at Hall of Fame Exhibit Opening." *Baseballhall.org*. The National Baseball Hall of Fame and Museum, 25 April 2009. Web. 25 May 2013.

9. Ibid.

10. "Aaron Wouldn't Change Record." *ESPN.com*. The Walt Disney Co., 14 Feb. 2009. Web. 26 May 2013.

11. "Recollections of Henry Aaron." *MLB.com*. Major League Baseball, 22 May 2007. Web. 26 May 2013.

12. Madden, Bill. "Hank Aaron Says Steroid Cheats in Hall of Fame Should Get an Asterisk." *New York Daily News*. Daily News LP, 26 July 2009. Web. 25 May 2013.

INDEX

Aaron, Barbara (wife), 20, 29, 38, 60
Aaron, Billye (wife), 9, 61, 80
Aaron, Ceci (daughter), 29
Aaron, Carolyn (sister-in-law), 44
Aaron, Estella (mother), 9, 17, 63
Aaron, Gaile (daughter), 29
Aaron, Gary (son), 29
Aaron, Henry "Hank"
  adolescence, 18
  after baseball, 77–84
  awards, 22, 27, 34, 36, 82–83, 92, 93
  childhood, 17–18
  children, 20, 29, 60
  death threats, 7, 11–13, 62, 63, 78
  divorce, 20, 60
  education, 18
  marriages, 20, 29, 61
  nickname, 9
  parents, 17
  records, 7, 11–14, 58, 60, 64, 69–70, 74, 77, 82
  retirement, 73–74
  trade, 67–68
Aaron, Henry, Jr., (son), 29
Aaron, Herbert (father), 9, 14, 17, 19, 26
Aaron, Lary (son), 29
Aaron, Tommie (brother), 44
Adcock, Joe, 29, 43
Alexander, Roger, 68
Alou, Felipe, 50
Atlanta Braves, 7–13, 46, 49–50, 52–54, 60–61, 64, 68, 73, 77, 79, 83
Atlanta Stadium, 7, 49, 50

Baker, Dusty, 60
bats, 33–34
Bonds, Barry, 87–94
Bonds, Bobby, 88
Boston Braves, 21, 25
Bragan, Bobby (manager), 44
Brooklyn Dodgers, 18–19, 26, 29–30
Burdette, Lew, 29, 36

Carty, Rico, 50
Cincinnati Reds, 13, 26, 34, 35, 43, 57, 64
Cleveland Indians, 69, 78
Cloninger, Tony, 50

Davis, Tommy, 44
Detroit Tigers, 69, 73
Downing, Al, 7–8, 14
Downs, Bunny, 20
Dressen, Charlie, 43
Drysdale, Don, 42

Gantner, Jim, 73
Garr, Ralph, 54
Gehrig, Lou, 30
Geraghty, Ben (manager), 21
Gold Glove, 36, 92
Grimm, Charlie (manager), 26
Gross, Don, 35

Hall of Fame, 19, 29, 42, 53, 54, 73, 80, 81–82, 92, 93, 94
Haney, Fred (manager), 33, 42
Home Run Derby, 46
Houston Astros, 50

Indianapolis Clowns, 19, 20–21

LEGENDARY ATHLETES

ABOUT THE AUTHOR

Doug Williams is a freelance writer in San Diego, California. He writes on a variety of topics for many publications. Previously he worked 23 years for the *San Diego Union-Tribune*, where he was deputy sports editor and sports editor. He's covered the Olympic Games, Super Bowl, Rose Bowl, and major league baseball. This is his third book. He loves spending time with his wife, two adult daughters, and golden retriever. He remembers watching Henry Aaron hit his 715th home run on TV and also getting the chance to watch Aaron play in person at Dodger Stadium in 1974.

PHOTO CREDITS

34 22